EXTREME OF THINGS

Books by Jenny Joseph

The Unlooked-for Season (Scorpion Press, 1960)

Boots and *Wheels* (both Constable, 1966)
(PROSE FOR YOUNG CHILDREN ILLUS. KATHARINE HOSKYNS)

Wind and *Water* (both Constable, 1967)
(PROSE FOR YOUNG CHILDREN ILLUS. KATHARINE HOSKYNS)

Tea and *Sunday* (both Constable, 1968)
(PROSE FOR YOUNG CHILDREN ILLUS. KATHARINE HOSKYNS)

Rose in the Afternoon and Other Poems (Dent, 1974)

The Thinking Heart (Secker & Warburg, 1978)

Beyond Descartes (Secker & Warburg, 1983)

Persephone (Bloodaxe Books, 1986)
(A STORY IN PROSE AND VERSE)

The Inland Sea: A Selection from the Poems of Jenny Joseph
(Papier-Mâché Press, 1989).

Beached Boats (Enitharmon Press, 1991)
(PROSE WITH PHOTOGRAPHS BY ROBERT MITCHELL)

Selected Poems (Bloodaxe Books, 1992)

Ghosts and other company (Bloodaxe Books, 1995)

Extended Similes (Bloodaxe Books, 1997)
(PROSE)

Warning: 'When I am an old woman I shall wear purple'
(Souvenir Press, 1997) (GIFT BOOK ILLUS. PYTHIA ASHTON JEWELL)

All the Things I See (Macmillan Children's Books, 2000)

Led by the Nose: A Garden of Smells (Souvenir Press, 2004)
(PROSE)

Extreme of things (Bloodaxe Books, 2006)

(Above titles all poetry except where otherwise stated.)

JENNY JOSEPH

EXTREME OF THINGS

BLOODAXE BOOKS

Copyright © Jenny Joseph 1986, 1987, 1992, 1999, 2006

ISBN: 1 85224 681 2

First published 2006 by
Bloodaxe Books Ltd,
Highgreen,
Tarset,
Northumberland NE48 1RP.

www.bloodaxebooks.com
For further information about Bloodaxe titles
please visit our website or write to
the above address for a catalogue.

Bloodaxe Books Ltd acknowledges
the financial assistance of
Arts Council England, North East.

Cover printing by J. Thomson Colour Printers Ltd, Glasgow.

Printed in Great Britain by
Bell & Bain Limited, Glasgow.

ACKNOWLEDGEMENTS

This book consists of a body of new work together with poems selected from *Persephone* (1986) and *Ghosts and other company* (1995), both published by Bloodaxe Books, as well as from *All the Things I See* (Macmillan Children's Books, 2000), and *The Inland Sea: A Selection from the Poems of Jenny Joseph* (Papier-Mâché Press, Watsonville, California, 1989).

Acknowledgements are due to the editors of the following publications in which some of the new poems first appeared: World Book Day anthologies (Macmillan Children's Books), *The New Humanist*, *Poetry Review*, *The Rialto*, *The Shop*, *The Times Literary Supplement*, and *You magazine*. 'Spastic letter' was published in *The Rialto* no.52 iunder the title 'Rock face in dark mist'.

CONTENTS

NOTE

The pieces I have extracted from my book *Persephone* to include in *Extreme of things* are not a continuous sequence in the original book, nor are they separate poems. In that book, different forms of verse and prose are juxtaposed, as voices in an opera counterpart each other, building up patterns of sound and rhythm that recur through the whole work. The old Greek story of Demeter's loss and retrieval of her daughter, which I have used traditional narrative verse to tell, is reinforced by prose accounts of scenes of modern life. 'Narrator's lyric' runs like a thread between the different pieces of verse and prose, giving some binding to varied styles. The lyrics are like beads dispersed at different junctures through the material on the thread of the whole narrative.

I am here reprinting in a group some of these beads, which being mainly to do with elemental happenings and changing seasons, seemed to belong comfortably with the direction of *Extreme of things*. Likewise, the poems I have chosen to reprint from *Ghosts and other company*, *All the things I see* and *The Inland Sea*, are not at all the only ones I want to preserve from those books, which remain as volumes in their own right, but those that, while being intrinsic to the volumes they first were part of, also seemed to be leading forward towards the new poems which form the last section of this volume.

from

GHOSTS
AND OTHER COMPANY

A chair in my house, after Gwen John

The house is very still and it is very quiet.
The chair stands in the hall: lines on the air;
Bar back, a plane of wood, focus in a space
Polished by dusk and people who might sit there.

Pieces of matter have made it. To get in words
What you could do in paint
Only the simplest sentences will serve.

And in this presence how much "elsewhere" lurks.
It is a sort of listening to the air
That laps the object, a breathing in of light
That's needed if we are to see the chair.

Here I pare this little stick of words
To keep away the crowds
And set my chair down, which words can never do.

The yellow daisies clash in the wind outside
It's not for long we can ignore they're there
Your noisy letters are dead in a box in the town
Your pictures breathe this wordless atmosphere.

The day goes through the room: dusk, white wall, through
To dusk again, and my wooden chair stands there.
I cannot get my chair the way you do
The things you paint.
Even the simplest sentence will not do.

Trompe l'œil

Old woman
Sitting by the fire
Making a lap from spread legs, and the scarfed outline
Of the little old body in the picture books;
Veined hand forcefully on knee to heave you up
From mental dawdlings mulling by the fire
In order to fetch something, to laugh, to make a rough crack,
Tough enough as old boots are to be capacious
For the lumpy foot that can fit none of the shoes
On offer in the shops; –
Stop being busy and practical for a minute,
Turn your head.
I've blown the cover you use for every day.
You can bring out now the small child from the folds
Of the air where you've hidden her about your person.
She is rising through the palimpsest
Of the way you lean and look and scramble up,
As a shadow strengthens at the strengthening sun.
There's still this young fruit, this kernel, this shape in little
From which the tree has grown,
Not child of your womb, or child's child that, separating,
Continued your life elsewhere, but – ghost if you like,
Pattern within the substance – rings of a tree
Still living in the wood for the eightieth year
To be there too.

You have withdrawn to look for something to show me
Leaving me in the company of a small bright child
Sitting by the fire heaving its cat in its arms.

Generation gap

'Where have you been, child, that took so long in coming?'
'Curled up in a warm place with the other animals.'

'Why did you not come sooner, while I could play with you?'
'My mother was playing, and had no time for me;

But you could have seen to the living. They had need of you.
If I were with you now I'd cry and be annoying.
You'd wish for peace again.'

'It is true, my twinkle, my apple of the eye,
That when you are born you will be wet and squally
And when you are growing I shall worry and complain.
But dreams are fed, my darling, on messy living beings.
It's contrary old people who have no use for pallor:
They want the sun, and comfort and real soft flesh again.

All that time you kept off when I could have been with you
Were you somewhere gathering merit, becoming beautiful?'

'Curled up in your mind, grandparent, keeping you company
And better there, I reckon, than a brat on this bothersome earth.'

Expecting guests

I have made a seat in the yard
I have clipped the hedge and swept out the corner
Of crinkly plastic pots, split, whose plants
Long since ceased to come to anything.

I have made a seat in the yard.
It is not a proper do-it-yourself shop one
But the seat and back of a broken chair I did not burn
Set level on some bricks I found by the path.
There's serendipity for you, a thing made
Out of things found, much the same as you are.

It is high enough for very short legs only.
Too low, this seat, for anything but small squatters.
When will you come and visit me, arrival?
You will like it here in your place that just happened
One happy day;
From chancy rubbish: an aimed arrangement.

You, floating past creeks, promontories, islands
Chancily washed into the flowing current
That is bringing you this landfall after all,
Visitant from the unmarked stuff that stretches
In every direction round our patch, where things
Become visible like the circle a lamp furnishes
Viewed from the dark,
Friend from the other side, before and after,
When, season's bird, will you come, alight
Matching your landing to the swaying branches,
Come and lighten, sunshine, the corner I have made you
And where I await you?

Skipping song
circular chain

Listen to the air
Hush babe
Let me listen
Listen to the thought in me
Babe in me

The edge of the circle flames with light
Hide babe
Like the after-image of a burning ring
Come babe
Mercury, fire that does not burn
Babe in me

Do not
Break the circle
Interrupt the beat
Or stop listening

The stone
Makes the ripple
Makes the circle

The movement
Turns the rope
Turns the air
In a circle
Dazzles on the air

The movement
Breaks the circle
The stone
Breaks the water

After-image of the circle of light
(Do not stop do not burn)
Child.
Child in me
Lean and listen
Do not interrupt
Child, thought in me
As you turn the rope
Move your arm
Make the arc thresh
(Again and again
Thwack thwack on the ground)
Don't stop, whirl it round
Make the arc whirl
Or the rope falters, coils
Dead snake, a dead snake
Dead rope on the ground.

Lean and listen, rapt
Do not interrupt
Child
Keep the circle
Flaming.

In a dark stone

'About seven thousand years ago
There was a little girl
Who looked in a mirror
And thought herself pretty.'

'I don't believe you. All that time ago
If there was a little girl she'd be wild
Wearing skins, and living in damp woods.'

'But seven thousand years ago
When England was a swamp with no one in it,
Long before the Romans,
In other lands by rivers and in plains
People made necklaces and learnt to write
And wrote down their accounts, and made fine pots,
Maps of the stars to sail by, and built cities;
And that is where they found this mirror
Where once the Hittite people roamed and ruled.'

'So you were there, were you, all that time ago
And living far from home, in ancient Turkey?'

'No, but I saw this mirror. Here in England.
It was the smallest thing in a large hall
Of great bronze cauldrons, statues, slabs of stone.
You mustn't think that it was made of glass
Common, like our mirrors.
                                    It was
A little lump of stone, shining; black; deep;
Hard like a thick black diamond, but better: obsidian.
It would have fitted in the palm of your hand.
One side was shaped and polished, the back rough.
Small though it was I crossed the room to see it.

I wanted to look in it, to see if it worked
Really, as a mirror, but I waited.'

'Why did you wait till nobody was round you?
You weren't trying to steal it were you?'
                                    'No. I was scared.

I waited and came slowly to it sideways.
I put my hand in front. It worked as a mirror.

And then I looked into that polished stone.
I thought the shadow of the shape I looked at
Was looking out at me. My face went into
That dark deep stone and joined the other face
The pretty one that used to search her mirror
When she was alive thousands of years ago.

I don't think she'd have come if there'd been a crowd.
They were all looking at the gold and brass.'

'I wish I could see it. Would she come for me?'

'I think the mirror's back in Turkey now.'

'I'd travel miles and miles if I could see it.'

'Well, nearer home, there were flint mines in Norfolk
And just where the land slopes a bit above some trees
On the Suffolk-Norfolk border, there's a track
And once I saw... But that's another story.'

Song

'Prepare yourself for death,' the old man said
And I, being a child
Crossed arms upon my chest
And said goodbye.

'Prepare yourself for life,' the preacher said.
Obedient as a child
I opened the window wide
And the rain came in.

'Prepare yourself for nothing,' my memory said
'Emptiness, silence, if I look to you.'
I turned the handle on the door at last
And walked through.

Paper tigers paper loves

Draw me a cat to frighten mice
Write me a love that has no ending
Fashion a flower out of gold
Send me a swan chiselled from ice,

And I will provide you with clockwork mice
A box for the papers the attic can hold
A jeweller's flower-bed that doesn't need tending
And a fridge from my heart to keep the swan nice.

The buried army at Xian

There have always been
Watchers in tombs
Slaves foxes thieves.
But do the dead still watch?

Through dusk of the day
I knew you were dying
A hedgehog emerged
On to grass I was watching
In the garden where I listened.
Dim hump where light was leaving.
The air was charged with portent.

The sand has drifted
Like drifts of cloud in sleep
A sleep of centuries

On some monuments
A beetle or a searching rat in stone:
Metempsychosis, or
The ravages of time.
Something escaping from the rot of flesh
The soul scurrying to next habitat?

Silent armies of the Emperor
Moving, cloth-shod, in twos and threes
    down passages
Converging for your last eternal duty
Phalanxes that gathered
Armed and in formation
Standing guard to warn the Emperor,
Your watch is eastward where the enemy
    comes from
Watching the night out, night of millennia

We have disturbed the sleep of the warriors
And made them stand upright,

As if
We were to plough the poppies in again
Trenching them back again into the earth
And make the revealed dead
Gather their limbs, settle their helmets on
Struggling upright in twos and threes in the ditches
(With here and there a fallen comrade leaning
As if asleep – on mud, or nestled on shoulder)
And stand to attention to salute the last post sounding

Against the pull of the ground
Their horizontal.

Lay them down, lay them down
Cover them over, unfix their staring eyes
Let them rest.

I'm standing late at night
In an emptied part of the city.
A small-hours' gust sends smoke from a
    brazier
Over a pile of sand at a fenced-off roadworks.
From grit and fog and shivers of tiredness
    emerge
Outlines of figures, wisps from the pile of
    sand
Dispersing down vague alleys of the air:
One year, two thousand, coiling up from
    the past
Push through the cover of time into the
    present.
The dead and buried are keeping their
    watch on the living.

You who will never be a ghost
It is your voice in this life that I hear
Not from the past, but as if you telephoned.
Egypt, the North, Mathematics, the stars,
As food and fags and drink and your good body,
Were pleasures to you, and to your end
The swagger of a good looker made you shine.
Beam of generous love, your fulsome gifts
Re-commended the world, all your geese swans.

I wander round London, I think I hear the phone.
It is I who haunt, not you.

The next July
Keeping the date
Keeping that week of your death
I saw the hedgehog.
I stumbled over him on the dark path among the buckets
And then
Never again.

Later, outlines of a warm October,
Through mist in valleys and in towns;
Lights up before shops shut, people,
Busy through the dusk, and the night
Inhabitable, not a separate country
Beyond the limit of our circle of light.
Through it comes
The soft insistent breathings of Hallowe'en.
                    The time of return – not this year's dead though;
                    Not recent ghosts these waiting warriors

                    Waking from drifts
                    Drifts of sand

                    Drifts of clouded sleep
                    Sleep of centuries

                    Silent phalanxes
                    You stand waiting.
                    In Christian monuments
                    The Dead awaken
                    Bodies assemble, reassemble, gather
                    A silent troop,
                    An army gathers under the sand
                    Beavering in the night
                    Night of millennia.

Weak torso falling, soldier on brother soldier
Head on his shoulder falling, going, so tired
Falling into the long sleep, sleep of the centuries.

Now light has prised eyes open
Like a jemmy a coffin
Treasure to peer at
Prising out the meaning
Dust falls as you open your eyes
You flag, you fall, you crumble

Later we found the shard of an old hedgehog
Carrion cleaned, thrown on a dump, not smelling
Flexible spine mat, cleaned white-skin underside
Dead and much like a doormat, pink underneath.

Cohorts all tangled, the lines all out of
    order
Chariots overturned, horses
Pulling over the shafts
As their knees keeled and broke

Leave them so
Cover them over
Let them rest.

You sleep on your side as the wind un-
    covers you
Blowing the sand shallow, life and the air
    destroying
As death did not, your perfect pose and
    order

It is an accident that you remind us
Of a tombed knight awaiting resurrection;
And something your makers could not
    know, that the plain
Devoted to monument, riddled with
    guards of the dead,
Had living armies marching over your heads
Before the clay was dry.

The hedgehog comes into view from a place of darkness
And then is found on a dump chewed clean by insects.
Goodbye, my friend; but you believed in this life:
It is your voice I hear, and your love that keeps me.

The new day, unarmed, leaves no holes to hide in
The enemy has been gone for thousands of years
The East comes in scorchingly with its bold blank glare

'Birth copulation death'

T.S. Eliot's Sweeney

Wrap me up and hold me close
A baby needs to feel secure
Against the pressure of the light
Against the drumming threat of sound

    Loose my limbs and let me go
    Flinging, open to the sky
    All the air within my lungs
    Every land, discovery

Hold me close and wind me round
Safe in a box of darkness, tight
Held and wrapped so I am sure
I'm back in the earth with Lazarus.

Flesh

1

If I held you round your little neck
And crunched the bones, then I could stop your life.
At other times this pulse and this stuff called skin
Could last out eighty years, eighty plantings
Eighty turns of the world itself.
Sheen, hair, vibration, the warm smell
Whiffle and pantings of life, eye and its apprehending swivel,
Flames its own substance –
Like magnesium dazzle
Like the burning bush unscorched.

All this would go, as the colour off a dead fish wanes,
If I put half an inch of my dead-skin thumb
Or a bit of any matter
Half an inch further in.

2

Little animal, little person
Skin tight across the bone, skin sweating
Eyes stretched and over them, shaped couverture
Little person, little animal.

3

Cat and me are getting old
See where it lies
As if it could not fold its limbs
To keep itself from getting cold.

Old man, old cat sitting together
Waiting; for what?
Something that will drop us both
Beyond the clutch of day and weather.

4 *Moon and flowers*

If there were flowers on the moon
And sharp and bright and eerie that would be
They would be like the laws of nature
Like the light from the stars.

But our flowers are rooted in colour
And they are mortal.

5 *Magnet of the well*

In the clearing stands a well
Round about it pathless woods,
Here, foolishly, the vague rabbit
Lolloped, floppied, ventured out.
Its strange long ears went down and down
Reflected in the black water
Blackness as dazzling as freezing headlamps.
Something pulled it harshly over
And the unrooted light green lace
Of duckweed that should have skimmed the surface
Coated and sank with it, and was dragged down.

A few *do's* and *don'ts* to help you care for your equipment

Give some attention to the face:
The fronting signboard of our lives and loves,
Starting position in the race.

Pay some attention to the hair:
Woman's glory, man's comfort,
Pulse of animal health gleams there.

Protect the vulnerable hands:
Agents of thought, tools
Intrinsic to the brain's commands.

Do not neglect your feet, for you
While you can walk
Depend on them to get you through.

Lift like a bowl your lungs, breathe in:
Only the pathways of the air
Supply you if you are to win.

Keep trim the ports and mechanisms
The eyes the ears the nose the skin
The portals where our *nous* homes in.

Tend the poor body as it's twirled
In time and space. It is
Your only gateway on the world.

Old night

There is a dark river called Chaos,
And it glitters, being thick and dark, with cusps of brilliance
Which make nothing visible.
To its bank even the sunny child
Destined, you'd say, for open meadows, comes.

No river of forgetfulness
Lethe or Acheron or tide that brings
Annihilation where all roll to rest.
No, this is the flood one, the Stirrer
The one that whirls rot, garbage
Suddenly above its banks, throws up
Defilation, broken things.
Equally swept to this littoral, shells
Of uprightness, the beaming surfaces
Of mother-of-pearl success.
Whichever road they were going they arrive at this shore.
Here good comportment stands with smiling face
Nevertheless for virtue come to this ditch.

You are weeping in some smashed place,
A place now used only for getting out of,
All its windows of light shuttered up, bedaubed.
Grit stings and greasy rubbish mires your ankles
As you wait in this sour wreck for shattered buses.
What has happened?
Your idea of your life
Our idea of a town –
Come to this?

Some think they can ride it as the skateboard boys,
Manipulating gravity, shoot out from dark tunnels
Balancing up into daylight on a wave of will
Their lithe persons now nothing but extreme desire.

But not this chariot.

Empedocles said that love comes out of Chaos
Twisting up and then unravelling the rope.
That unsorting the elements, muddling the order, mixing
Gives the momentum from which love leaps, as the spindle
Twirling back up the shaft, winds and unwinds.
But I do not think that love is why the dark glitter
At every turn of beauty pulls us down:
As blood threads flesh this wild and greedy dark
Veins existence.   Fighting the elements
Is what has made us human, and doing so kills us.

Some would say:
Ride the rails then, swing and catch the trapeze bars,
Jump on the bumping cars, run off, twist the handles
To crash into the next, leap off laughing
And dodge the lumbering furies;
Like the graceful ne'er-do-wells who cavort and slap
Their boards about on concrete under the walkways,
Leap to the arms of the magnet your iron is set to,
Ride the lurid glitter, the spume of the dark.

By Lake Huron in winter

Day dies on Huron – huge marginless waste.
Last gleams catch crests of ice scummed over dunes
That merge with the frozen rubble of the lake.
No earth, no water; ice and the whipping wind.

And as it darkens at the edge of the world,
Up there, up there in clarity of sky
Sun's flash, off metal no doubt, and a golden track
That hangs there a little after the planes have gone.

On devastation bent perhaps they fly –
To bomb a southern city, conflagrate.
Fire, first of the elements, is the fiercest, farthest
Most absolute in destruction;
                              and yet

Earth water air without the aid of fire
Remain forever sterile. The atom of carbon
Chained in the leaf awaits the flash from the sun
To set it going and make the rabbit run.

from

ALL THE THINGS I SEE

The things I see

Hurry hurry hurry
It won't do you no good though.
The lights ahead are red
You go up to the slap bang
Rocking on your chassis.
Meanwhile you have missed
What I have seen –
A small boy hiding behind a tree
And the buds breaking out all around him, kissed
With little tongues of green.

Angry angry angry
It won't do you no good though,
For the catch on the door will slide
When you push your boxes through at that hasty angle.
The red fuming skin of your face
Must be all your eyes can see.
Meanwhile you have missed
What I have seen –
A woman with a strange patched face
Looking up into the spring sky through the mist
In her light eyes, for Heaven's Queen.

Furry furry furry
It won't do you much good though
To be wrapped so warm to the eyes
That you cannot turn your head
That you miss what I have seen –
All the things I see:
A tall man like a pole
And at the bottom of his long arms, down at his feet
A tiny little pushchair and a tiny baby
Sunk in its hammocky seat between the wheels;
A little girl sitting high up on her father's arm
With a long furry tail laid heavy among her ringlets
Swinging from her Davy Crockett hat;
And two extraordinary pigeons
Of quite different and glistening colours.

And a cloak of St Francis brown and a Mary's blue
Walking together collecting the dust of the street
All the things that I see
As I hurry hurry hurry
To work, but slowly, slowly.

Coming up our street

Everything is news to me
The grit on the pavement winks with a new eye.
The angle of the building never signals the same way twice
As I turn round it home.

What face will be looking out of the picture this time?
What voices call when I open the twice-read book?
The future is tucked in corners with the past
The air is loaded with things we have not in mind.
So I turn round the corner, the last before I get home
For there is the house appearing much as I left it
Its outline still real against my bit of the sky.

Getting back home

Hang your hat on the peg
Rest up, rest up
Fling your coat on the bed
For you have travelled many miles to see me.

Put your feet on the bench
Rest up, rest up
Heave off your heavy boots
For you have come through winter days to see me.

Settle down by the fire
Rest up, rest up
Lean back and smile at me
For after all this time and travelling
Oh traveller, I'm glad to see you.

Humans and animals

It would be nice to be a bird
And not mind the wet;
Not to have to scrunch up,
Not to have to be brave getting into the river:
Holding our breath, screwing up our eyes, flinching into a jelly,
But to continue with our purposes like the horse
Who grazes at the same pace in an open field
When arrows of rain fall thick, silvering
The pall which obscures the meadow as it comes down.

Towards the end of summer

Cherry red and honey bee
Buzzed around the summer flowers
Bumbled round the luscious fruits.
Patient weaver clambered by.

Silently while the others bobbed
And busied in the bright blue air
Hither, zither, merrily,
Weaver waved his cool brown arms
And gently drew around the tree
Silken skeins so fine so fine
No one could see that they were there,
Until one autumn morning when
Cherry was gone and bee asleep
A silver shawl was laced across the grass
With little beads like pearls strung all along,

Legs like a friend of mine

In front of me on the pavement suddenly your legs
(Long ago friend)
Legs with no ankles, plonking firmly on
(I push through the crowd)
One set of toes turned in a little bit
(I call your name out so as not to miss you).

I get round to the other side and too late to halt my greeting
An ugly face looks crossly into mine.

My friend from long ago, you would long ago have told me
It is not considered a reason among grown-ups,
To say, when one embraces a stranger,
'You've got legs like a friend of mine.'

Changes

My butterfly brooch is flitting off
Through the open window;
The hedgehog from the hearthstone moved
Sure though slow;
The bird in the picture on the tree
Has gone, and the real sea
Must have taken back the crabs and shells
We put in the pebble-filled watery jars.

Where, you ask, have our creatures gone?
They moved away when you left home.

Sun and rain: Yes and No

Standing on the platform
Waiting for the train
I look into the puddles
Made by the rain –

Made by the rain falling
Into the dips in the ground.

I see a bit of blue sky
Beyond a castle wall
And a shimmer and sheen of green leaves
Waving over all

Then rain splashes break my picture
Falling without a sound.
The rain says no to that castle
But the sun says yes.

I look back from my puddle
And see the station wall
With groundsel and other weeds
Straggly and tall

A concrete pillar was my castle rock
A green poster my trees.

The country in the puddle
Is changing again
A great foot has stepped in it
And here is the train.

The speed makes up the picture
Of any station that I know
And the sun shines shouting 'Yes'
Though the rain says 'No'.

Looking at pictures

I would like a walled garden with flowers hanging
In cascades down white-washed pillars in the sun.
I would like hounds an leashes.
I would like not to be me.

But if I lived in a past age and had another body
Perhaps I would look *out* of this picture book and think
'I would like a world where babies did not die, where
Children were not whipped and where people believed what was true.
I would like not to be 'important' and afraid; to play in the street
And laugh without hiding bad teeth and have clean hair
And go in for my tea when someone called, instead of ordering it.
Oh beautiful tough and lucky little children
I would like to be *you*.'

Poem for an old enemy

Although I did not like you, Monkey Puzzle,
Thinking a tree to be a lush and shady thing
In the green England I grew up in,
Finding your iron spikes not right, too bold
On the lawn of my childhood,
Dusty Monkey Puzzle Tree
I regret your passing.

Seeing you in this other garden I go past now
Every day to work, I am reminded –
I am reminded of the surprise
Of thinking of trees and plants that were not green,
Without a smell or soft moist earth round roots;
Of a tree, not-a-tree, that must always have been old.

Now here I look as usual from the bus
One morning, and don't believe – but you are gone.
And why should I be sorry, who never liked you
Personally, Monkey Puzzle Tree?

Because I remember the hours I spent looking
At your crazy branches, trying to find the way
If I had been a monkey, that I would have gone.
And so your dingy and depressing arms
Still make me think of the courage of persistent people who pit
Human wit
Against impenetrability.

Another story of Hare and Tortoise

There was something I forgot to tell you when I told you the story
Of the hare and the tortoise. You remember,
How the one animal, splendid, desirable, eager
Life tingling in its limbs, was admired by all
And how the other
Arrived when nobody was actually looking.

They said it was his desire to win – obstinacy,
Nobody else was there. He said he got there.
We were all gathered round the starry hare
Succouring his weakness.
(His faint was only a lapse; he was a splendid runner).
But even if it's true what tortoise said
We were not there to greet him at his win.
The world had gone elsewhere
We wanted to be with hare.

The loneliness of saying 'I won' to nothing but emptiness!
He wasn't liked. He worked for what he got
And always so damned fair.
It was much more fun with hare.

Zenith: hold it

Cuckoo long gone
Summer heat upon
The land;
Harvest not yet come.

Waiting, who knows for what
To happen, at the spot
In time
We have arrived at.

If we could – Stop momentarily.
Let ourselves be
Held, moveless, in the turning hub
Of eternity.

from

THE INLAND SEA

Bonfire

An hour or two till dusk with the wind fallen
We lit the fire, collecting all the junk
That over the months had soddened into the corners.
We swept the yard of crumpled leaves and sweet papers
Dusty and rotting.

'That'll never catch, all that damp soggy stuff
And the stench will be awful.'

Suddenly there shot up a flame
Very bright and clear through the coiling rolls
Of oily smoke, and it seemed to burn up the smoke;
Bright, inimitable, worth it.

Then as unaccountably it died.

Ash is everywhere.
Now it is dark
And none of this black ruin will light again.

Redistribution

They sat on the polished floor and ate up the huge orange
He had left for his wife.
They got the skin off with his special spring screwdriver
Rusting it, although a fruit knife
Lay in its place in the drawer. On sheets of paper,
Cream linen, kept in a box for the fairest of fair copies
They scribbled little notes and added up,
And used, to unblock a drain
A slender silver pencil he had gone to great trouble to get
Engraved with her name.
Allowing this misuse of her prized possessions
Gave her a sense of freedom – no hoarder she
Of having been fondly thought of in retrospect.
They ripped through the velvet substance he had gathered
With such gloomy care
And walked out guffawing and loving into the sunshine, leaving
        the French windows
To bang and shatter in any storm that came.

For C.J.
In his late eighties

Old man
Do not fear to be
A dirty old man.

A stone doesn't smell
A stone is warmed by the sun
And then goes cold.
If it smells of heat
It is not its own,
If it smells wet
It is the seaweed's life.

The sun goes in
The seaweed rots and crumbles
And the stone is there.
What does it supply in its purity, giving off nothing?

What feeds us rots, and rots us.
You have risen to the smell of young flesh
Your body has been sappy enough to become old,
To exhale age, like cupboards, to be unsavoury
As happens to flesh, (though not to yours as happens);

But your thoughts,
Your intentions – that side of life you could choose –
That you can keep as clean and cool as a stone,
A stone settled into the sand shining at the sea.

One that got away

This little old lady I meet
Has nothing to do with poetry
Coining home late from work I pass her
Say once a week, maybe it's a Thursday.
She is entirely dressed in red
Not garish, though, not bizarre or fancy
And not at all a tramp.
Tiny, smart and silvered. She's still pretty.
I am going home from work, and she
Is coming from goodness knows what –
Pub, dustbins, cleaning – no knowing.
And I could not ask her.
She has nothing to do with poetry
And she has nothing to do with sociology.
Social workers may be out looking for her
To divide her into classes
Doctors to separate her into diseases
Politicians to flatten her into statistics
Poets to dispose of her in images.
She is not to do with any of that.
I did ask her once 'You all right, duck?'
First time I came on her, sat on a low church wall.
Surprised, she seemed – as if she wouldn't be all right!
She has nothing to do with horror stories or signs of the times.
Here she comes with her small packed carrier bag.
I am not going to tell you anything more about her.
She makes a track going here and there
Inhabitant.

from

PERSEPHONE

Autumn, Winter

The summer had been ended for some time
If not officially
Before the shock of greyness, blanketing,
Pressed the blind season up against our faces.

Winter, my God, a familiar I had forgotten:
That's all I needed.
The portcullis dropped and locked around our houses.
The long worthwhile campaign to build the town up
Surrounding it with fruitful fields was seen
To have been only a little flourish; frivolous –
The house of straw of the pig before the wolf.

'The dark is back,' the eyeless morning said
'The wide white dawns and evenings when the girls
Were out in the meadows gathering at every hour
Are blotted out. They are not beyond the horizon
Waiting their turn to be brought back with all their flowers
When the ball heaves them round, like clock figures
Wheeled to the front when the hour strikes. No horizon
Nothing but a flat plate filled with fog
Jammed in a sphere no breeze can pull apart.'

'So be it, morning of my dearth,' I said
Deliberately got back into bed
Gathered all heavy covers I could find
To blot the nothing out, hiding my head
And sank into the nothing in my head.

Then
Close in my ear a blackbird called its song.

Turn back
Turn
Back into the shell
Turn
Back down between thin grasses to the earth
Turn away
Turn from such light as there is
And cover your head in a small space
Creep
Creep into the blankets
And sniff, with eyes shut, for the salt and stale smell of the bedclothes.
Creep down between the humps of unwashed covers
Heave them above you. Sink beneath the floor
Sink, comatose, shred-winged fly, in the stagnant
Water of the neglected tank
Sodden with cold, inert with slime, airless.
Shrink between cracks in the wall like a woodlouse
There lie curled
The eyeball turned on itself, turned and stuck there.

Turn back
Turn away
Creep inward
Burrow, but not forward, only
Down, in, under
To the dark, to join with the dark
As desperate body clings to unheeding body
Through the black vacuum sinking separate shaking
In a grasp as hopeless as the blank clutch of lust.

We look at the grass and say, when it is brown,
That is nothing of us, stray wisps,
Flaccid bits not now separable
From the mud they're plastered in.
And even at times when it is green again
There looks no sap, no coolness of life to stroke
The fever off from the skin of the face, no salve
To oil the skin of the hand to growing again
Through crusted sores that metal and hard things caused.

Not without struggle, not without falls and deeps,
Winter has caught us.
Truly a lifeless field under this wind –
This grass never flesh.

Does the dog wake thus,
A heavy curtain clinging round his heart
Dust of betrayals lining his memory?

The blanket of the morning shuts the sight
Within the house, and when at last the light
Struggles down brown passages of air
The street, curtailed by winter, hostile, is all that we see there.

But does the dog wake like this, or the crow?

And how does the animal die?
In fear, no doubt, galloping across the field,
Struck in mid-flight, but alive until his death?

The days grow smaller and the freezing night
Tourniquets volition. The day
Returning is impotent to repair
For at our dying, unclenching the hand all that we find there
Is 'Does it matter if we know?'

On the bush emptied by autumn one fiery leaf
Hanging, embalmed; bare dead branches else.
On the bush by the wall one leaf, and one bird;
Who now for the last time calls his cry
Telling some master of the approaching change
Calling to some other kingdom news of withdrawal,
Telling of closure, of sinking, of even that leaf
Fading to sodden earth.
The earth is dun and the last colour going
Yellow leaves in the bush, sparse, sapless
Like the hair of a fading girl.

The drowned man rolled in the wave, his eyeballs fixed
Staring for spring in the stars through yards of water;
The fledgling crushed and cat mauled, the dead sheep
Shuddering for summer in a wall of snow;
The worm making backwards to the warmer regions
Finding dark earth, static, airless, unheaving;
The axle broken and the fixed stars fallen,

The clutch of ice, the blown brain, the spilled heart.

The horizon, lethal with cold
Pretty and pink and lethally cold.
The pink dies into brown and disappears
And the cold curls up from the ground, and like a breath
Settles from a low sky, and the afternoon snaps
Off into night.

Summer child
Where do you go in the winter when nights are dark
And the ground sodden?

I saw a fly
The sort with long drifting legs, clambering among my ashes
Left from a warm season.

Brown-legged skinny cotton-clad dancer,
And summer drifter –
I had forgotten I had forgotten you
So closed this season.

Spring and Summer

Unease
Wind of March,
Halting
Then upwind from the track the noise of shunting.
Look up, straighten up, see
Swirled branches, swirled clothes in yards
Tugged at, tugging.

Light at strange times, rooflines
Seen in new positions, then sinking;
Echoes sounding from further than yesterday,
Heads lifting.
You find yourself walked two miles from your room
For no reason
Tasting time in unknown parts of the town
Turning this way, that way, stopped before windows
Uncurtained, though still the shut-in season.
Unaccountably women scrub out drawers
Men are late home
And when they come their wives
Are turning things over in high parts of the house
Not crouched in the kitchen.

And suddenly you are reminded there are backs to things
As when the light is switched on behind the gauze
Backdrop that has blanked our sight till then
And the prince goes down through the wood to another exit
Brick wall till then.

A child plays out after dark
First time this year, and you hear:

She is coming
From the paths within the woods
Up the gulleys from the plain
Drumming drumming
Insects building citadels
Bud-sheaths opening with a jerk

61

All wing-folded creeping things
Heaving up to gasp the air
Thrumming, thrumming
Tricklings, juicings, fattenings, breathings
Sighings, heavings, spreadings, reachings
She is coming; if you listen
Spring is here.

Oh no, I do not believe
As the snow swirls again and the windows
Drip from the inside taking the warmth from our breath
I do not believe;
As the black lines creep back through the newly faced walls
I do not believe;
Dead letterbox, telephone, eyes down, arch filled
Doors shut, blinds down all day, gate locked, lease ended –
I do not believe.

Something is gathering at the edge of the meadow.
Do you not hear
The bird calling across the wet grass
The bird invisible singing from behind thick air
The blackbird's whistle carried by the rain?

I have heard –
Out of the empty season, weary August,
When for a stagnant month no call has broken
The bronze and heavy sky –
I have heard suddenly a blackbird sing
And the next thing we knew the year was dead.
Crying within walls I have heard the warning,
Blackbird's alert, Hades' bird to tell him
Prepare his riches.
                    So I do not believe
Not while this damp and still clings round my head,
This heavy emptiness afflates my heart.

The steam outside is thinning against the stained windows
The houses and trees beyond stand out and come nearer
Somewhere she is moving, prepare to receive her.

A cold fury has snatched at the little edges
The unfurling of the lime buds, the ragged wave of the elm leaf
There are shreds, silk scraps of leaf from the woods on black pavements
Purposely pulled apart as when, torn to scraps
A page of a book is destroyed.
Shoots looking out for air are broken, fronds smashed
Harsh whirlwind is up there, black storm clouds with hard edges
No vague-sided clouds bringing softness, bringing liquor
Balmy for growing, soothing and hushed exhalations,
Like velvet nostril quivering, sleeping in hay.
Foolish greenery may have arrived out of habit
But the pellets of ice are coming, and black rain to cover it
Bowing down everything and driving it back to its cave.

She is not here. She is nowhere here. I do not believe.

It begins to be light
When the child comes home from school now
Lingering in puddles, satchel banging knee.
The fir tree stands still behind him
The moon and the sun stand still in the light blue sky
The moon pale, its edge mouse-eaten like cheese.
The sky is pale, like crystal, without heat
Indeterminate, like a girl waking.

The earth turns
Carrying its slugs and singing birds and light,
Bringing to the surface all its buds and shoots
Its fledglings in new nests and baby mice.
The softened warmer side comes uppermost
Hard black clay and icy silent waters
Tilt underneath, waiting another year.

The earth turns.
It brings the twittering children, and the birds,
Busy brown creatures, chattering freckled waters.
The infant stretches to the strengthening sun
The infant stretches, sensate, wakening
And, widening with the flowers his star black eyes,
Turns with the earth out to the year that opens.

You see this rain
Slanting out of a copper sky
Falling from the middle of the air
Not higher than the trees or buildings
Immense light still bright behind the edges
And the woman in a sunhat running out to save the washing,
And you hear it, how it soothes with its gentle patter
The crinkled earth:
Big soft drops you can separately hear, splashing;
A black rag flaps across the corner of the eye –
Blackbird homing from green –
And this rain is trickling down gulleys, into the splits
Of hard old tracks, stamped hard with sorrowing feet
Cracking with weariness and desiccation.
And if a seed, pushed by the winter wind
And rotted as a useless wisp of hay
Is licked into the light and rained upon
There stands your wheat.
Rain, you are loosening something in my bones
Soft fingers draw back coverings in my head.

Something undoes with a little lurch, rose
Of blood opening in the body
Body that pumps these rivers of the world –
Torrents of love to make the grass grow,
Persephone's moist breath in the rising corn.

O tiger, O leaping animal
Skin that the sun reverberates on,
Green lancing sticks whirling the air that lies
Bright white about your points
O repetition
Of birds for the first time ever heard,
Persephone out of the house of darkness:
Sun, voices, spring.

Slowly the drop collects.
One more ooze of liquid and it will be
Big enough to make a sun of the light.
Slowly the pool fills till the brim is reached
Echo of trickle in basin is gradually dimmed,
Sharp edge of the sound of water dulled in fullness.
Gradually the lake rises and spreads out its silk
An open eye within the secret hills
Fed silently by many secret waters.
Slowly the fish in the lake swells and the skin stretches
Become a bag of eggs when the light touches it.
The peony loosens and the sunflower turns.
The noon swings and stretches, keeping
The dark a long way off at each end of the day
Far, far,
And even at midnight the fishes feed and swim.

Slowly the drop collects and carefully
The spider travels daylong to and fro
All summer building.
We look at the field path near the edge of dream
And pause like someone coming out of a wood.
In a minute the fields will shift into focus
With a path to walk on through the long 'now' of summer.

Blind window flashing from the roof
Looks out towards the unseen sea
(Beneficence of iodine
Carried inland on the southern breeze)
As a face is tilted (eyes elsewhere)
Up to the sun, up for the grace of love.
Heavy with summer's apogee
The trees are hanging in distant squares;
Petrol and tarmac shimmer there.
There is no hope, but no more need to hope.
The long note is held quavering
Stick on a drumskin is still.

Second Autumn

In those days in autumn when it is fine
The brick of the old church is such a red
The house next to it white, such a white
Ultimate, and the paint extreme of black.
The essence of all substance stands and declares.

Babies turn and look at their mothers
Boys lie on turf with dogs on no restless business,
Traffic waits without swearing, with open hand
As if to say 'Pass by, pass by you all
I, only guardian to wait and hold.
The beautiful girl, a joy – she is not searching,
The ugly old, relaxed, are not bitter.
Nobody barges into any other;
Day's fulcrum at the point before the year plunges.'

We have not thought to expect anything further
Yet as we unbend from looking at the grass
Moving too quickly, slightly giddy from the blades
There is a luminosity, world of light – gentle:
We catch it as we straighten.
Though some of the grass is brown, it is rooted
And the mud it is rooted in gives off this light
That swells out from the patch of herbage, and shines
Up at the red brick walls, the paint, the washed sky,
And the eye that looks stores up the life for it –
Part of it
Grass become flesh and flesh exhaling light –
As the seed
Which keeps the tree entire within its thought
Holds the strength for the plant against the season
We all know is coming after this day dies,

On the bush touched by autumn one fiery leaf
Blazes a clarion, calling across the sunshine;
On the bush by the wall one fiery leaf and one bird
Calling; announcing an approach, slowly from a distance.

Messages go out like an arrow over the wood;
Gather your strengths now, harbour them together
For soon a busyness, a stir, a progress
Will arrive at these portals, collecting from all directions
To pause before the tunnel wind absorbs them
Mustering for the journey to Hades' halls.

Draw the curtain on their room
So that the moon's long fingers, broken
By thin cotton, shall not harm
These beautiful beings of the sun,

Warm and soft and animal
Almost fragrant to the mouth.
Let a little moonlight in
So the night air comes and goes
Not shut up, not spirit sealed,
But protected, made at home.

Heat of day and year, has passed
Dreaded dark is yet ahead.
Cold but fruitful harvest moon
I dim a little of your light
Lest too soon you make my children
Creatures of your glittering night.

Look through the pane
What do you see?
A person moving
Away from me.

Look on the hill
What do you see?

The sap retreating
Down in the tree.

Look on the meadow
What is there?
The grass shrivelling
Dead like hair.

And on the road
That leads to the farm?
The place is shut up
The people are gone.

On the bush emptied by autumn, one fiery leaf
Hanging, embalmed, bare dead branches else
On the bush by the wall, one leaf and one bird
Who now for the last time calls his cry
Telling, who hears, of the approaching departure,
Telling of closure, of sinking, of even that leaf
Fading to a listless earth
Dun-coloured, dimming; see, the last colour is going
Yellow leaves in the bush, sparse, sapless
Like the hair of a fading girl.

The ragged wind
Pulling the skin off the clouds, stripping
The seed heads from the stalk, emptying
The blue mirroring gutters full of water;
Hauling-down wind
That broadcasts and let fall handfuls of sorrel
Dry-pulling with a rough finger
Scattering on to the soft earth that even under this cloud
Shows colour from its moisture, that reflects
Not high blue heavens, but leaves and seeds and shoots –
Loot that the wind has dropped –
Little green spears like fuzzy mist on the ground,
Mirror of spring.

On the bush emptied by autumn one sapless leaf
Hanging, forgotten, bare dead branches else
On the bush by the wall one leaf – or perhaps a bird
Silent and still, as dusk thickens to dark.

Through the wall of glass, wall of solid water
Figures of people. People talking? Not hearing.
Figures turning away, gesturing weakly
To others who do not see: drowning
Open-mouthed in horror – but no sound.
Glass or water or ice, clouds. The people are gone.

I went back up to bed on that dark morning
As the fog rolled in, and under heavy chill covers
Curled up in misery, my face to the wall
In a room in one side of a crumbling house, in a corner
Jammed up against the side of an empty building.

Nothing stirred within, without; no hours
Moved, and nothing happened to tell me
Of any life or stir, or that there ever would be.
Perhaps I dozed or merely, blanked with numbness,
Let time fall.

Then suddenly I heard him, a blackbird
Showing, I suppose, quite natural next to me
On the other side of the wall, then, there was air,
Space, movement, and a blackbird calling somewhere;
Telling Demeter, if she could have heard:
Do not, O mourner, look in the summer fields
They can be nothing but symbols of barrenness now;
Life's attributes are shifted to the grey wall
A little green lump of moss and flirting of wings:
The herald sings above the gaping hole
Opening to a black tunnel through the wall.
Do not you wait in a barren field that the sun
Once touched but has no power with now.
Here is the power
And here the new life harbours.

69

Ah, once again I hear you, Hades' bird
Unmarked these many months while the young girls played.
Now he calls, beginning his new time
Suddenly quite near after long absence,
The bush that holds him bare of any cover
And yet I do not see him for the dark.
There again, quite natural next to me,
The blackbird sings, staying close to the wall
Summoning, drawing, so that I turn again –
Herald, harbinger of real adventure
Calling all together for procession
But he stays near the cleft in the wall, the hidden tunnel
Stays and declares, calling beyond the dusk
Calling to the flocking ghosts, and the wraiths that dissolve
In the short dim day, singing that the earth may mourn
And all on earth may shrivel and be sad
But not for her, for she has escaped earth's death.
Leaving, she fades into power, wrapped in Hades.
Mourn, he calls, mourn for Demeter, mourn
For your poor cold hearth, your loss, your diminishment

But as for Persephone, as for Hades' bride
Why, she goes down to riches.

NEW POEMS

I heard the cuckoo

I heard the cuckoo and I saw him fly,
And that is in my town dreams as I lie
Up in a block whose lights reduce the sky;

As when, to some steep lane, shady and long,
Because I have been, once, part of the throng
Come thoughts and faces that I've lived among.

Echo and Narcissus

Do you hear me call your name
Across the years?
Do you look across the street
As I pass?
Or
Up the bare field frosted
In the light
Dying further after a short dark day
Follow
To where the town is fringed and edged with trees
And the cuckoos and the swallows in the summer
Used to come and go,   and I
Used to walk and hear it clearly, hear your name
Rising through my heart
Do you ever listen for it now
Your name?

Of course I hear a name
Across the years
And sometimes catch a movement
In the glass.
But
Learnt long since that these,
Like you dear ghost
Fumes from the carcasses of dead desires,
Come
From wisps and exhalations (as a breath
Pushed into frost reduces, and, steam to water,
Wets the edge of a scarf)   and I
Trudged, tired out, the other labyrinths, seeking
For different longed-for voices
Haunting and listening, longing to hear
My name.

A child taken out at night for the first time

My father said my little sister
One week old today
Although a perfect healthy child
Can neither see nor say.

I saw a picture of the earth
A turning ball that shone.
The Tellyman said it was the same
As the flat earth we're on.

My father took me to a field
In winter after tea.
We walked away from the road – he said
We needed it dark to see.

He put his finger under my chin
So I looked up. The cars
Were far away behind the hill
And *I* could *see* the stars.

The luck of life

There was a lucky boy
And he lived in a house.
His room was painted silver
The door: brown and green.

There was a lucky fox
And he lived in a wood,
Just on the edge of it
In a sandy bank under trees.

There was a lucky rat
And he lived in a pipe
Half-buried in a building
In the middle of a town.

There was a lucky snake
In a biscuit-yellow place.
Miles and miles it stretched
With rocks for shade to sleep in.

All these things were charmed.
Their luck was the air they breathed.
They lived sometimes in danger,
Sometimes they played in peace.
They slept or they scurried,
They moved and breathed and ate.
There was colour in their houses
And firm earth underneath.

The magic of the brain

Such a sight I saw:
An eight-sided kite surging up into a cloud
Its eight tails streaming out as if they were one.
It lifted my heart as starlight lifts the head
Such a sight I saw.

And such a sound I heard.
One bird through dim winter light as the day was closing
Poured out a song suddenly from an empty tree.
It cleared my head as water refreshes the skin
Such a sound I heard.

Such a smell I smelled:
A mixture of roses and coffee, of green leaf and warmth.
It took me to gardens and summer and cities abroad,
Memories of meetings as if my past friends were here
Such a smell I smelled.

Such soft fur I felt.
It wrapped me around, soothing my winter-cracked skin,
Not gritty or stringy or sweaty but silkily warm
As my animal slept on my lap, and we both breathed content
Such soft fur I felt.

Such food I tasted:
Smooth-on-tongue soup, and juicy crackling of meat,
Greens like fresh fields, sweet-on-your-palate peas,
Jellies and puddings with fragrance of fruit they are made from
Such good food I tasted.

Such a world comes in:
Far world of the sky to breathe in through your nose
Near world you feel underfoot as you walk on the land.
Through your eyes and your ears and your mouth and your
        brilliant brain
Such a world comes in.

That's life – or it ought to be

I am the sort of person who dogs bite
Of whom their owners say
'But she never bites anyone.'

And you, the other half I'd like to be
You come along as the bus draws up
And jump straight on.

I get to the town just as the cafés are closing.
You keep both gloves, together, in a drawer,
Or if you drop one, it's there when you go back.

Together we are called 'day', 'life' or 'it'
But life's hard on me when we are separate.

There are too many...

There are too many cats in this book.
There are too many cats in this garden, say I.
There are too many cats, says the dog,
We will get rid of them.
And the bird fluttering from the ground says 'Yes and you too.'
There are too many dogs in this town, agreed the cleaners.
Get rid of them and their muck and their unhealthy ways.

And the pale lettuces bemoan the slugs
And the snails the many boots that crush them regardless of their
        beauty.
There are too many pigeons, say the owners of pea-fields
Too many sharp beaks, say the soft-curled caterpillars.

And insects, oh insects, say the people swatting the flies,
Picking spiders out of their baths,
What need for so *many* too many? Get rid of them.

There are too many people says the earth
Too many of them dumping great loads on me
Weighing me down, covering me up, erasing my creatures.
I think I will give an extra strong shrug and heave them off,
These noisy squabblers, these tinkerers and complainers.
I will get rid of these far too many people
So I can breathe again.

Spastic letter

When we had come to the impossibility of words
We resorted each to our own desert.
So further and further the tiny figures go
Into hallucinations, like dolls in fever.
The silence clamped the heat waves to the horizon.

There had been times
When silence was different, not out of gloom but joy
(Like a child nodding and beaming into a telephone)
The air too full for words, pulsing, breath held
Presuming the message carried.

But then we got to where what seemed the path
Veered into nothing. There was a rock face.
There was a murderous gorge, dark mist arising.

Blocked by the unreal, as thoughts are
That have no journey out but only speak
To their distorted echo boxed in iron,
I accepted that was all there would be, ever.

How to get back from that place? Well, as in dreams
The differences in life are not explained
Though we spend lives trying to. For no reason
(I mean no virtue of mine) find me,
On a dim locked day, dull; nerveless;
All there would ever be: empty, forever –

                        And suddenly there was a bird singing
In such a shout of voice
As if the world's strength of huge waters
Supplied that half-inch throat a kitten could throttle.

Bird, sing for me.
Muse, little bird, I will be careful,
Not moving too sudden as you hop at a distance.

Muse, sweet song.
You come at your need not at mine.
Do not wait too long before you visit.
The smell of the turned earth, or you spotting
Some movement of succulence in it
Has drawn you
Beady eye, sleek creature, swift flyer.
A sad heart, like clamped soil, is no good to you.
Do not leave it too long before you visit.

Meanwhile, you I cannot speak to, accept
A potent silence.
Words have their uses, they will come again
Perhaps at times less needed. Meanwhile
My talking to you when you are not here,
With ease and clarity in the room I've made
In my own mind – where we sit together
Or stroll about the streets on summer evenings
Listening to the bands – will not reach you.
But as the muse of love, the lively bird,
Filled my blank air with its unbidden shout
Perhaps in the room you have where your ghosts come,
Within that silence, perhaps you speak to me.

Lullaby

Only when we are in each others' arms
Babies or lovers or the very ill
Are we content not to reach over the side;
To lie still,

To stay in the time we've settled in, that we've scooped
Like a gourd of its meat,
And not, like a sampling fly, as soon as landed
Start to our feet,

Pulling one box on another, Ossa on Pelion;
Getting the moment, only to strain away
And look each day for what each next day brings us:
Yet another day;

Pleased with the infant's health and the strength of its frame
For the child it will grow to,
The house perfected, ready and swept, for the new
Abode we go to,

The town in order and settled down for the night
The sooner for the next day to be over,
The affair pushed straight away to its limit, to leave and notch up
Another lover.

Lie still, then, babies or lovers or the frail old who
In dreams we carry
Seeking a place of rest beyond the crowds
That claim and harry.
We are trying to reach that island for the festive evening
Where our love will stay –
Waylaid, prevented, we wake as that vivid country
Mists into day.

Stay on this side of the hill.
Sleep in my arms a bit longer.
This driving on will take you over the top
Beyond recall the sooner.

Exody

There it is, some heat, some source of love
That we, turning, move into. Daylight
Is not the sun coming up, warming our world
But the earth turning.

Nor does love and its beneficence depart,
Its outline a cape drawn slowly across the ground
Its shadow swallowed by the horizon.
It is we who are going.

Water widens between slow ship and wharf
An imperceptible movement, more swell or drift
Which cannot be rated by the people on board
Except by their hopelessness.

The last to be seen of people thus moved away
Are their backward-reaching arms,
Stretched to their limit against the tide's momentum,
Failing to touch the handhold of the sunshine.

Better to think it so, that the source is there
And we are taken away to the shadowed side
Drawn to the iced quarter,
Than how it seems to our senses, than how it feels:
That the sun itself it is that comes, and has gone
Leaving us grieving, helpless in the dark,
For what will not come again.

What brings words up

What brings words, what brings the voice up
From the locked hollows of the heart?

Love has its own wordless answer, mooning about
In converse with its object: secret, silent
Words for the beloved are wrapped in entrancement
Of its own imaginings. It listens, not exclaims,
Hearkens to a rounding within
Of gleeful happiness.
The cat has got the cream so feeds and waits
And needs do nothing further.

Even when love's subject is away
Gone to another world of its own preference
It is not love that forces out the cry,
That pushes words out like a waterfall,
Pours words on to the page as a waterfall
Perpetuates torrent,
Not love, but longing; longing and desire
That sends the walker down the roads at evening
To stand where the bank rises, looking to the west
For the last of the light,
That makes migrating birds call eerily
Out of the sunset; that makes us cry out
'Oh, love; love.'

Love meanwhile is sitting cheerily at home
Tying up plants, enjoying
A hundred humdrum jobs; to the outward eye
Not moved, or wrapt, or loaded.

Sometimes overcome as if at a pause
Leaning against a wall in the middle of another action
We say a name, not in plea or prayer,
To anchor a presence, as one might the shape of a cat
Slunk to its hearth when not expected:
'Oh, cat,' – as to say
'There you are.'

Headlong through a day we stop on occasion
Fully to attend a child's tugging,
Waiting on its urgent claim 'Yes?' we ask.
Then there is nothing it can show or say.
The need is that we stop. They cannot say
'Be where I stand, look out at this with me
Your hearing curled in my ear. Be part of this and me.'

'Listen,' I say in my head.
'Look, love,' as if the air
Can spread through time as well as across space.
The wind, dumb messenger, has not left its cargo
At the address, nor stopped to pick up any missive
In return across the years.
It whistles on its own journey over a land
Where telegrams and paid replies
Are as unheard of as any messages.

Looking up from my book that has taken me down
To the mind and places where I feel a current
Suasively friendly pulsing that mind to mine
As if two people were meeting, talking
'Listen, love,' I say, 'how about
A walk before tea?'

A child rehearses vocatives
Or up against the window strains for the moon
To clear the clouds so it can shout 'Look!
You can see the moon now. Come and look.'

The good didact points out
'If you have a command, a plea, or question
In a piece of writing it doesn't mean there is really
Another person with you in the room.
It is a ploy, a good one
To summon up the presence of a person,
Second in this case, the first being understood
Behind the command,'
(As prayer is not for some thing, but so the choked heart

Can unblock the fallen slurry and make a passage
Setting up a connection from the need
To have something to pray to, as if a leap
From a crag top, into the void, will cause
A soft little eyelet of grass on the other side
To rise for us to land on).
'The vocative's rhetorical.
Rhetor, the official persuader for mercy, in the Greek courts,
The oldest name for what a poet does.'

Let us start again... you there, me here
With pen and paper trying to give you answers.
'What do you see, what are you thinking, what
Do you want to say?'   And I
Have all the world moving around my head.

Look love, at this light...

And 'Look,' I want to say, a ghost on the wind
A wind calling, carrying messages from a land
As used-up as the star from which the light,
Reaching us now
Evokes a breath answering 'ah' as we look at the sky.

There is nothing to see here you don't know already.
You have trees lights shadows stars, effects and new creations.
If you came to watch over my shoulder
The nothingness to your eyes would make it crumble,
Nothing left I could really want you to look at
Better than where you are where these same things
Mean more to you.

The only thing left to hear is me saying 'Listen'.
All that's to see is me asking you to look.
The years have emptied out the store of savings.
What the wind carries to the clod is empty husk.

No love lost

'No love lost between them,' the saying goes.
Ah, but love *is* lost.
In ponds
           it is sunk;
In woods whose solitary drippings on dark days
Encased us in our miseries, it is buried.

Think of a favourite place
An angle of a wall
A café where friends meet
A window on the street
A particular field walk
Known to you from childhood
Where you have taken your dreams
And made them resident.
You go to tend them there.
Later you take your beloved
Into the haunts of your heart.

The pool, become a secret source for you
Shown as a view is stagnant and nondescript.
The woods your thoughts and days inhabited –
Leaf-fall sifting into mould and mast –
Are tedious and disagreeable to push through
By someone come there with different expectations.

You thought you would say
'Because I brought you there once when we loved
Something of us together will remain,
Something of secret joy will still suffuse
Drab days in the inert world.'

What rises from the place is the dismay
The deadliness and gloom of the walk back
From the place spoilt with the wrong visitor
And shame remembered at the invitation;
Love buried and lost.

Lost but not found there if we visit later
There, where we linger, trying to retrieve
Even our sorrow, even the absences;
To mourn, not love now but the life of love, the ardour
That immersion in love fired up.

That sharp life, as solid as a tin
Buried with a note beneath a doorstep,
Neglected has thinned and faded.
And what we could not get out of our system,
The pervasion we could not flush from our thought and blood
(As an after-image seems stuck inside the eyeball
Preventing us seeing where we are),
Has melted into wisps that drift away
Thinning like aeroplane trails, dispersing
Into invisible air, far far beyond calling,
No memory of trace at all in the wide sky.

But what is found, what lasted, kept its savour?
Something not looked for perhaps when love was wanted.
Something found to have grown but not when, consumed
With unbearable sadness at life-blood wasting away –
Our life cataclysmically destroyed –
We looked for returns from such loss.

In history the Destroyer came quite often out of the North
The Mongols, the Vikings, shafting South –
Lines of terrifying horse-heads cleaving the plain
Prow-beaks cleaving the water.
On the north wind also came the dust
Yellow-grey soil, ground out from the edge of ice sheets.

The Huang-he, crystal at source, flows through North China
A thousand million tons of sediment in its yellow belly
Slowly, sluggishly past the huge loess plateau, Yellow River to the
        Yellow Sea.

Loess came from land dry and windy, treeless.
Aeons of grinding of wind of water
Of piling up and sinking back
Made grains, finer than sand, into rock.

To geologists it is 'recent' – New Pliocene.
They can date it because of what they have found in it:
Fine calcium carbonate tubes running vertically
They think derive from roots of ancient plants.

The Huang-he silts up, its bed thickened and raised,
Truly an overground river like an El carrying traffic
Above the fields, the banks, the huts, the farmers, the towns;
And annihilates three huge provinces; of all unpredictable rivers in
      the world,
Called Ungovernable.

Layers laid down,
Which present times flow over.

Layers of living laid down which make a past
Our present runs over; the substance reinforced
With mesh spreading out like a root system, grown
From actions that keep life going;
Skills learnt and engrained speck by speck by the doing;
Ways we make by walking them.

What survives? What lasted?
Freed from the personal, the wider tract
Out from the dire crags to the open plain,
Less stunning, but a clear slow outlook
Where gradually those who stay there see the prospect
And the light of morning makes visible the filaments,
Modes of inhabiting which after years
(Not too much put on them, nor much examined)
Are found to have woven a fabric after all
Which clads what was down to the bone; a wrap, a web
From which a garment is formed;
And what was lost and which produced such pain
Has filtered through the substance, leaving deposit
Of what was waste, was rubbish
Become a feeding source, absorbed, discarded,
Built up, turned over, turning lives over
In land, far distant now, from the habitation
In the wide country we have settled in.

Health

We are sound when we are well with friends.
To love and be loved is the very state
Of our thriving.
                    Our luck: to have reached that acme
We had not thought for us.

There are pools
Fishes and campers come to in the moorland streams,
Sudden cessation of the tumbling roar,
Where a widening of the space the rushing water
Has carved between rocks, holds the water level
In a perfect round; and keeps the canopies
That grow from the rocks, cliff high above our heads
A little apart so that the light comes through
And shows their mirrored counterparts with sky between
Steady and placid blue on the deep quiet bottom:
Rock, light brown sand, washed by the liquid light,
Shafts of sun and shadows
Moved through by dapplings, fish and dartings
Of fish, and slowly sinking leaves,
But in itself not stirred.

It is a warm flame when we are well
With those we love.
It is the climate
Of pleasant living which nurtures
Goodwill, good deeds – civilising virtues – that grow
From the give and take of errands. They substantiate
Kindness, concern, attention, notice taken:
Receiving which we can in turn take part,
Our actions part of the social hum of days
That tells us the generator powering this network
Is ticking over nicely.

What we had thought could only be a respite –
Access to a lighted place on a dark road
Welcomed for a rare holiday, dipping the toe
In a life quite different from our own
Which we go from rested, salved, furnished

With wider knowledge to help us on our way,
Refuelled with energy that being liked has given –
Became a place that, arriving as a stranger,
Was recognised as home, made for us, and which
We could take part in making, our visitor's offering
Accepted.   Our liking
Received.

Not nomadic in our affections, we think:
'This can be my life now; and recognise
We have reached the condition, told us long ago
Was the success to aim for: a place in the linked chain
That joins us into human commonalty –
Our proper life and what we have been made for.

And so in pleased surprise we settle.
The trajectory is completed. The arc of it
Curved down to its resting point:
As stones bed down
Into the soil they're thrown on, become hard core
Grown down to be part of the landscape.

We acclimatise
To the good weather which spreads beneficence; rely
On amity – received, returned –
And take it as base not bonus.

A stream hurtles from the moorland.
Over rocks it tumbles.
Ditches, rivulets
All feed it
Unitl it becomes a stretch, sheltered, held in.
This is what they make for,
The swimmers, the picnickers, the boaters.
Here they drop their gear
And do not think of looking further.

Unaccountably the season changes.
Suddenly that the others have lives elsewhere –
Always had – is apparent: more central to them

Than this we bask in and make the grounds of our being
And which is now, for them, peripheral.

They are pulling in from that outer circle, they are packing up.
There is no room for anything more than their own needs,
Which have surfaced as other than ours. Damp in the air
Makes lines in plaster stand out through layers of paint,
And like the side of the moon we cannot see
When the lovely shiner makes beautiful our night
Our existence has become blank to them.

So that's the end and home is lost, life finished.

As if the summer had been our habitat, without its ease
We cannot exist. The first sharp frost
Blackens to ruined stalks the half-hardy plants
And we are as ended as the season's creatures.
Nowhere to go, no way of staying. Finished.

The pool fed by the rainbowed waterfall
Is not a closed lake. The water from it
Leads to the open plain,
Joins the river and becomes the name
Given on maps and in the memories
Of people who live along it.

There is a route on, to the lower reaches
Though harsh and wearisome.

Life pared of all extras, down to endurances
All worn away save mere endurance,
Down to the skin and bone, is yet time's clothing.
The skin that covers time
Becomes our life's skin, and the layers' accretions
Make time habitable.
The deprived body goes on doing all
That flesh is set to do, including to grow,
To be tough, to survive, to clad itself, to wear.

As we go further, sometimes changing direction,
Points in the past

Swing to a new focus behind us and gradually
We may do alone what we learnt to do in consort.

Tougher than we had thought or wanted to be
We continue through the populated land,
All its processes waxing, waning, turning.

We with it, scarred but hale.

In Memory of Philip Stone

All over any small garden there are thousands
Of webs, of silk trails, the different formations
Of one or other out of a possible six hundred
Sorts of spider.   In winter
Few are visible but they are there.

You may take your torch
Searching one spot, for a key dropped perhaps,
Or on a day when light strikes a dazzle of diamonds
From a thick wet hedge, get one whole and perfect
Made in a flash.

Spider silk is incredibly tough and spiders
Reconstitute at great speed to repair ruins.

Something in the clinging fuzz that repels
Our fingers, picking out from corners of drawers
A disgusting ball of dust,
Healed fevered wounds when they used to bandage with it.
This same coating it is preserves the web.

Walking a short-cut path from the shops
I hear crying behind a hedge
(Run to see, pick the child up
Find its Mum, take the child home?)
Then round the corner comes
The child held tight by its mother
Still crying, still upset and angry
But crying within the bounds of safety.

Later the abysses of grief –
Dismay like a river widening –
Cannot be crossed by an arm round shaking shoulders.
To grown children we cannot rush
Encircle within our arms,
Pick up, hold tight, console.

Something happens: snow falls
Or the fog blows back.
We are in another place than we had thought
And we see some things in the dark winter garden
We had not known were there.

The gossamer patches discovered with a new day
May have been there a very long time, as may the carcass
Of some animal that autumn, night and winter
Snow-leaded weeks of dark   and fog
Hid, and whose habitation and progress through its life
We knew nothing of.

Those we love
We hold moments of, illuminations
Kept delicate and whole even when
The land is consigned to winter and the dark,
And no one seems to go there, and there seems no movement
At all under the iron cold sky.

Extreme of things

There was a man
Or it could have been a woman
(Accoutre them with such gender as you wish
Equip with such attitudes as you know of,
With such parts as you would like to imagine
And, since you must, think personally,
But at the extreme of things I doubt such measures matter)
Who against the storm had built a shelter.

Got it so he could dry his tatters
Got it so he could even sew comforts:
Cloth to prevent snow sifting through the lintel,
A quilted bag to stop the sand and scorpions.

WIND: My breath will outlast yours.
         All the sand and show is under my wings.
         I can drive it over the earth to you
         Even the long way round,
         Even if it takes a hundred years.

SUN: I can suck every drop of dew up, every river,
         The sap in each blade of grass streams towards me.
         Your pitiful shade and plants sizzle and shrivel, vanished
         Like a drop of spittle on a stone in the fire.

So trekked back, he or she, got family job place;
Wove a network, sat in conference, planned, entertained;
Made as many fences as Robinson Crusoe did who made
Fences to protect his fences.

'My breath,will outlast yours,' said the wind.
'I shall bleach your bones wherever you die,' said the sun.

Survivor's song
(New Year Blues)

On the last day of the year
An old year, a vile year
I walked into the town.

I walked into the town.
I saw by the fence, huddled, a mangy dog
Dog huddling, or maybe dead,
At the far end of an empty lot
Litter strewn; up against the fence litter choked.

I walked out on the last day of the year.
Ailing, been ailing a long long time
And the year was ailing, guttering out in despair.

I went on and the dog shook itself and lolloped off.
A door in a concrete shed opened and light spilled out
Showing puddles of oil and details of rubbish on the ground
And the gritty wind carried voices and some music with it.

I walked on into the town; felt nearer for the voices
(Ailing, been ailing now a long long time)
And I trudged on to where there were shops and busy people
And buses going home and people in them
Who were not all dire and dying and crying woe.
People were dumping their children and parcels on café chairs
(Slapping the crying child), talking to their friends, eating
As the year was guttering out, as the year was leaving.

And I thought: if I carry on and walk far enough
The child will grow up, and the lot be cleared of its rubbish.
I will walk through this time to another as some (though not I)
Walk away to a better place that is clean and comely.
I will walk till the road is better and the going stronger.
There will be things to notice apart from the ailing.

Ailing, been ailing now a long long time
But going still, walking on into the town
Walking the old year off and another one in.
Silt pushed by wind forms banks at the estuary
For birds and men; some habit of travelling
May take us through the gate of the time that is coming
As the habit of moving has carried us out of our past.

Elemental – not to mix, but how then?

The principles of anger and of blenching
Are best not switched. How sick, as shrinking violet
Tiger grin is. And obdurately wasted
The sallow forest windflower's silk skin lifted
On crag to face the noon.

The principles of rashness and of paleness
Are best not mixed. How useless in the foray
The sickened stomach of a decent fear.
Ruinous is the jewelled web as stanchion
Where a crude timber would support a door.

The balance of a milligram brass measure
Is nothing but curio in a sand-bagged city
And worse than curious, to weigh air in the desert.

We are brought up to bend mix modify,
We have to, to be human. We are not tigers
And even children with skin as soft as petals
Do not prosper if led to live like flowers.

So we fall twice, hubristic for purity
Rigid for the splendid idea.

To know and move on this
Is counsel of despair – and of survival.

A man draws a straight line

A man draws a straight line,
Incisively but even so it is done soon.
He is not so much drawing a line, though we describe it so.
The pressure of the balls of his thumb and finger,
The evenness of the movement of his wrist,
Take the mark along; at once a line is there.
But the weight of his body is behind that wrist, those fingers,
Thirty years' thinking has accrued within his hand,
The muscles pushing the hand inlaid with years of practice.

'There,' the man says giving the sketch map to his friend
'That's the route to take. See you Thursday.'

A child says 'Hello' to a new friend,
He has tossed for three nights worrying off sleep trying to devise,
Trying to find the right words to carry his meaning,
How to get across the chasm of this desire, this dare,
As you search restlessly for the best place on the bank to jump from.

He will be, like the big boys who toss clear words in passing,
Cool adult casual. Then his friend will like him.

The child mumbles a stuttered 'Hello'
Unnoticed by his tall new friend, the heroism unheard.

After weeks of fevered rehearsing a child says 'Hello'.
A man with paper and pencil draws a straight line.

Such is the sea

Such is the sea you cannot catch and keep it.
It never will be old, though it's always there.
Stand at the edge and throw a pebble in it
The heaving waves are the same as they ever were.

And such the land that, go to where the earth is –
Leaving the beach, scrambling across the sand –
There's a track between ditches, houses, then a river,
Flints in the ground you can take into your hand.

And you might find a place where something in it –
Shards that you finger – were the very ones
Discarded by the people who made tools
With delicate cutting edges, from the stones.

Such is the sea nothing can mark or map it.
Veined with time's tracks and remnants, such the land.

       . . . .

It was a rather empty stretch of heath
I came to once, a slope up from a wood,
Pits with flints in the walls, an uneven wind,
The setting sun in cloud, and an anxious mood

You cannot hold time, for time is like the sea
Washing all round us, but can hold a stone;
And you might feel the same as someone thought
Who, wanting not to be caught by the dark, alone,

Went scuttering down this track, and suddenly stooped
To pick a shining black bit from the ground,
Ground that holds vestiges of what has lived
Solid with time, itself to transience bound.

Such seems the sea to those who are not of it
But are the stuff of earth,
                  and such the land.

Jenny Joseph was first published by John Lehmann in the 1950s. Her first book of poems, *The Unlooked-for Season* (1960), won her an Eric Gregory Award, and she won a Cholmondeley Award for her second collection, *Rose in the Afternoon* (1974). Two further collections followed from Secker & Warburg, *The Thinking Heart* (1978) and *Beyond Descartes* (1983). Her *Selected Poems* was published by Bloodaxe Books in 1992, drawing on these four books. Her later collections are *Ghosts and other company* (Bloodaxe Books, 1995), *All the Things I See* (Macmillan Children's Books, 2000) and *Extreme of things* (Bloodaxe Books, 2006). Her popular poem 'Warning' (included in *Selected Poems*), was separately published as an illustrated gift book by Souvenir Press in 1997.

Her other books include: *Persephone* (Bloodaxe, 1986), winner of the James Tait Black Memorial Prize; *Beached Boats* (Enitharmon Press, 1991), a collaboration with photographer Robert Mitchell; a book of prose, *Extended Similes* (Bloodaxe Books, 1997), and *Led by the Nose: A Garden of Smells* (Souvenir Press, 2002).

She lives in Gloucestershire.